# Helping

by Terry Miller Shannon
illustrated by Susan Reagan

Mom says, "You can go to work with me today."
I love to help Mom at work!

Mom is a vet.
She helps animals that are
sick or hurt.

Some animals are pets,
and some are wild animals.
I help take care of them.
I help walk the dogs.

I give food and water
to the animals.
I clean their cages and beds.

I help lost pets find
their owners.
This makes everyone happy.

Sometimes wild animals get sick or hurt.
Mom makes them better.
We take them back home.

This is a good place for
animals to get well.
It is a good place for
me, too!